523

WAYS TO BE

AWESOME

by Kathryn Thompson

CREATOR OF *DROPS OF AWESOME*

FAMILIUS

Published by Familius LLC, www.familius.com

Familius books are available at special discounts for bulk purchases for sales promotions, family or corporate use. Special editions, including personalized covers, excerpts of existing books, or books with corporate logos, can be created in large quantities for special needs. For more information, contact Premium Sales at 559-876-2170 or email specialmarkets@familius.com.

Library of Congress Catalog-in-Publication Data
2015955953
ISBN 9781942934394

Printed in the United States of America

Edited by Stephanie Yan
Cover and book design by David Miles

10 9 8 7 6 5 4 3 2 1
First Edition

For the lady I heard
publicly thank her family
for loving her "in spite of
all this" as she gestured
toward her entire self.

INTRODUCTION

awe•some /ˈȯ-səm/ *n* **1:** your tiny bits of goodness that make you amazing **2:** every little effort you make: You're overflowing with Drops of *Awesome* today! — *adj* **1:** inspiring awe **2:** very impressive **3:** the way you are every single day of your life

I can think of five reasons you may be reading this book.

1. You are my mom. Hi, Mom!
2. You already know you're Awesome and enjoy reading about yourself.
3. You don't yet see how Awesome you are and hope this book will either help you recognize your inner Awesome or give you ideas about how to increase it.
4. You read *Drops of Awesome* the book or *Drops of Awesome* the blog post, and they were in no way offensive to you, so you're back for more.
5. You were given this book as a gift and thought it would only be right to crack it open.

Well, you've all come to the right place—especially you, Mom. I like you the best.

Drops of Awesome is a concept that was born out of necessity when I realized that often when I'm doing the most good, I'm hardest on myself. I tend to focus on whatever I'm struggling with, and then the one thing I'm not doing well becomes the focus of my life. *You made an effort? It should have been bigger. You cleaned the counter? It should have been the whole kitchen. You listened to your daughter talk about her day? You should have done that yesterday, too.*

One day, I decided to stop focusing on what was wrong and start focusing on what was Awesome.

Drops of Awesome is the concept that every good thing we do is a Drop in our Bucket of Awesome. Throughout the days and years, we accumulate these Drops and our Bucket fills. However, we can only feel joy if we recognize and celebrate our Drops. If I'm doing good things and feeling discouraged about my efforts, I will eventually stop doing good things. *If I'll never be good enough, why try?*

The more time I've spent dwelling on what's right in my life, the more I've found that I *am* enough. I am more than enough. In fact, my contribution to the world is kind of epic. And as I've seen myself more clearly, I've been startled by your beauty as well.

It's funny. You'd think that recognizing that you're enough might cause you to sit back and coast through your life. But I'm finding the opposite is true. The more we realize how remarkable we are, the more we are willing to experiment with new and different ways of being Awesome.

I've spent the last few years of my writing career working to convince myself and others like me that they're good enough—that what they do matters—and that if they will simply grasp the full extent of their goodness, they will increase in Awesome at a rate they had previously not thought possible.

This is my battle of choice in the war on negativity. The enemy, sadly, is not some distant foe. The enemy is staring right back at us in the mirror.

On a recent school visit, I was speaking to elementary kids about being Awesome and being a writer. At one point, I gave them a worksheet and asked them to write down one Drop of Awesome, one good thing they'd done that day. One sweet little girl looked stumped. She was about six years old and neatly dressed. She had been sitting quietly and attentively throughout my thirty-minute talk. And she couldn't think of a single good thing she'd done that day.

"It doesn't have to be big," I explained. "Just write down one good thing, any good thing, you've done."

Nothing.

From the outside looking in, I could see Drops of Awesome pouring out of her. She was attentive, polite, and sweet. She had treated me with respect and smiled at me. She was kind to her peers. Earlier that morning, she had risen, dressed, and made it to school. She had a pencil in her hand and was ready to learn. These were just the few things I could see at first glance.

But she could see none of them.

Why do we have a blind spot for our own Awesome when we can see it clearly in nearly everyone around us? Maybe it starts with modesty. We don't want to brag or be pompous. Maybe we're scared, afraid to own who we are, the full us, to glimpse what we're capable of and then be responsible for achieving it. Mostly, it has to do with insecurity and comparison.

We compare things that have no business being compared and come to nonsensical conclusions. *She ran a marathon Saturday, and I played Settlers of Catan all weekend. I suck.* The marathoner could just as easily be thinking, *She spent time with her kids this weekend playing games, and I selfishly ditched my family to pursue my own fitness goals. I suck.* My hope is that we'd both be pleased with our own offerings and happy for each other. However, I know from experience how easy it is to feel beaten down by comparison.

All around us, we see people doing astounding things. They invent technology and heal diseases, compete in elite athletic competitions, and create soul-nourishing works of art. We are amazed and inspired and sometimes intimidated by them. Next to their triumphs, we feel inadequate. And it's not just the Nobel Prize winners who make us feel this way. There's also the mom next door who runs past your house at five every morning, *and* works sixty hours a week, *and* coaches soccer, *and* keeps an immaculate house, *and* always looks like she stepped out of a J.Crew catalog.

In the back of our minds, we know that she's not perfect, that looks can be deceiving, that we don't know the whole story. But from where we sit in our pajama pants in the front seat of our minivan or from the window of our apartment where we live alone, our perception of her makes us feel somehow less.

And that's okay.

Yeah. That's right. I said it's okay. We notice differences. Sometimes we compare. Sometimes we're hard on ourselves or others. The Drop of Awesome in this is recognizing that we're doing it and then choosing our way out of it. If I notice my coworker's amazing ability to stay on top of email when I feel like I'm drowning in pixels, I can feel bad about myself or I can choose to be impressed. I can also remind myself that I'm excellent at in-person meetings. Seeing his success online can give me hope that it's possible to navigate this sea of electronic communication. If I want to, I can even ask him to share his inbox-management processes with me. Or I can just feel like crap. (There are many options here.)

Let's think about those big, epic success stories: the Olympic athletes, the billionaire entrepreneurs, the gurus, the What I Want to Be

When I Grow Ups. How are they different from me or you? In all the ways that really matter, they're not.

Just like each of them, you are a miracle! Your life, your breath, the blood moving through your veins, your skin that heals itself, your smile that heals others. There is not a single other person on this earth like you. There are things you can do, impacts you can have, that no other person who was ever born can replicate. If there was no you, the world would be less Awesome.

You are Awesome.

Do you know it?

But wait, you think, *I've never set an Olympic record, built a company from the ground up, or been a renowned guru. I can't even imagine what that would feel like!*

Can't you? Haven't you done many of these things . . . a bit?

I've created a list of twenty mind-blowing Feats of Awesome that I would love to accomplish, and throughout the book, I've written all kinds of Drops of Awesome you may be doing already or could do to capture the feeling of doing something amazing.

Here they are:

- Achieve world peace
- Compose a symphony
- Save a life
- Rob the rich to feed the poor
- Explore the galaxy

- Win an Oscar
- Make your first million
- Make an epic comeback
- Paint a masterpiece
- Raise a happy family
- Build your dream house
- Cure cancer
- Experience the greatest love of all
- Start a nonprofit
- Discover a new species
- Start a religious movement
- Arrest a criminal
- Earn a college degree
- Invent a new technology
- Win an Olympic medal

Reading this list may have brought back fond memories of your third grade essay, "Why I Want to Be the Dalai Lama When I Grow Up." Maybe now you suddenly want to jump in and achieve one of these goals. But before you sell all of your possessions and start gathering disciples, consider *why* you want to do it.

Why would you want to achieve any of these amazing feats? What are your motives? Do you really want the life of a religious leader, a full-time humanitarian, or an elite athlete, or do you simply want the feeling you get from doing the things they do?

For example, when I say I want to "discover a new species," it doesn't mean I want to leave my family for months at a time, live in the jungle, become intimately acquainted with poisonous insects, and document frog excrement. I don't actually want to be an explorer. What I want is to be more observant, to be closer with nature and other living things, and to experience the joy of discovering something new and sharing it with others.

So how do I get those explorerly feelings and experiences without the leeches and malaria? I start by recognizing and celebrating that I'm already doing some of the things an explorer does, a few of the things that help me feel what she feels, things that give me a similar feeling of accomplishment. Then I choose a couple more things to do.

When I list things like "Lay out your clothes the night before," I do not mean "Lay out your clothes every night for the rest of forever." I really just mean you could get a Drop of Awesome tonight by laying out your clothes once. I also mean if you laid out your clothes last night in preparation for today, stop reading for a minute and celebrate! By prepping for the next day, you added peace to your life and a Drop to your Bucket.

As you do these things, not only will you feel Awesome, you will *be* Awesome. You will find that you *are* an artist, or a scientist, or an inventor . . . a bit. You will be doing a little of what they do.

You might think: *Sure, I'll be doing a little of what they do, but will declining to share a juicy*

piece of gossip really achieve world peace?
Will drinking water today turn me into a gold
medalist?

Think about it. Isn't that what epic heroes do every day—save the world a little and then wake up the next day and save it a little more?

A symphony isn't written overnight and neither is your story. You are writing it one chapter, one line, one word at a time. What word comes next? Are you truly recognizing the words that are already there and the beauty they contain?

I feel confident that throughout this book, you will find many things you are already doing but haven't yet considered to be Awesome. I hope you will find many more things that inspire you to use the small free moments in your life to let your upward momentum carry you forward.

If you turn this book into a checklist and use it as evidence of all the things you're not doing, I will find you, give you a big hug, and gently pry the book from your hands. Because obsessive perfectionism is less than Awesome. Because you don't need that in your life. And because I don't know you individually and couldn't include every amazing thing you're already doing in this book. We don't have that much paper.

So even more important than doing any of the things on these lists is recognizing the things you are doing, whether on these pages or not. Celebrate your own Awesome.

Consider picking a fun-colored pen and marking the things you've done. Write additional things in the margins or on the lines at the end of each section. Make this book your own. (At least, I hope it is your own. If it's not, return it to its rightful owner. That's a Drop of Awesome!)

> If you'd like a more in-depth Drops of Awesome journaling experience, check out *Drops of Awesome: The You're-More-Awesome-Than-You-Think Journal*, available on Amazon.com and Familius.com.

THANKS

I want to give a huge thank you to the fabulous readers who contributed ideas for this book. Their Drops of Awesome are starred (◆) throughout.

- Linda Bittle
- Sarah Hardy Cardell
- Liz Clark
- Debbie Crotts
- Peggy Duffy
- Liz Gossom
- Myla Johnson
- Marsha Steed Keller
- Katie Roberts Murdock
- Debby Neal
- Colleen Pace
- Halley Pace
- Sina Johnson Penrod
- Jana Rinard
- Abbey Romney
- Timothy Steele
- KayLynn Thompson
- Kasey Tross
- Keri-Ann White
- Alicia Williamson
- Roslyn Willoughby
- Jen Thueson Wood

ACHIEVE WORLD PEACE

It's hard to shoot for a huge goal like achieving world peace if you don't have peace within yourself and with the people you know and interact with every day. Do you do things to bring yourself and others calm, peace, and happiness? So many things can be included here. Anything that makes the world better contributes to its net peacefulness and joy.

Breathe.

*Slowly breathe in and out, concentrating on the
movement of your own breath.*

 Let someone else be right.

Gain perspective five minutes at a time.

*Ask yourself if what you're doing right now will
help you be happier in five minutes. How about ten
minutes? What should you be doing today if you want
to be happier tonight? Tomorrow? A week from now?
If you want greater peace, love, and happiness in a
year, what could you do today to make that a reality?*

Don't fight back.

Do fight back when it really matters.

Choose to forgive.

Stop everything you're doing and just be.

Being is so much better than being busy.

 Eat your next meal slowly.

 Speak softly.

 Anchor yourself in the present.

Feel the texture of the surfaces around you. Smell the air. Notice your safety and peace. You don't live in "What if?" and "Maybe." You live in here and now.

 Say "No" to a request for your time that won't bring you peace.

 When you're not sure what to do, stop and listen to your heart.

Living a life in opposition to your truest feelings is living a life in opposition to peace.

 Let someone merge in front of you.

 Let someone else win the parking-spot lottery. ✦

○ Return your cart at the grocery store.

○ Return someone else's cart.

Several times, as I've struggled to load overflowing grocery bags and wriggling kids into my van, a stranger has offered to return my cart. I always feel loved and have a renewed sense of gratitude for the goodness of people.

○ Lay out your clothes the night before.

○ Don't mention it.

If someone has made a mistake and you find yourself repeatedly bringing it up, choose not to. Choose to let the other person grow, change, and move on. Think of how much you'd love that mercy to be extended to you.

○ Swallow a piece of gossip that you hear.

○ Listen at a time when you really want to talk.

○ Find an uplifting news story and share it with someone.

○ View your day like a home movie, with nostalgia and gratitude.

I love home movies and watch the most mundane moments over and over again. Life is better when you stop and watch what's happening around you with the same rapture and attention you'd pay if you were to rewatch it five years from now as a home movie. Laugh when your baby spits carrots all over your face. Listen intently as your kindergartner tells the lispy story of how his tooth fell out. Watch the moon rise over the ocean. Pay attention to your mom's story about when she was a kid.

○ Hug a loved one longer than you normally would.

○ Let someone go in front of you in line.

○ Choose not to brag, one-up, or hijack the conversation.

◊ Smile at the lady whose kid is having a fit in Target.

◊ Smile if *you're* the lady whose kid is having a fit in Target, and be thankful it's your kid and not you who's melting down. WAY less embarrassing.

◊ Think of how it could have been worse.

When I played Madam Bonbon in The Nutcracker, *I stomped on my five-year-old daughter's fingers and she refused to come out from under my giant dress and dance. The way I finally found peace about this mini catastrophe was to imagine how much worse it would have been if I'd stepped on one of the other little Bonbons' fingers. Things could almost always be worse. Be grateful for the way things are now.*

◊ Tell the mom or dad of a special needs child that they're doing a good job. ◊

◊ Tell ANY mom or dad that they're doing a good job. ◊

💧 Turn off your cell phone for an hour.

💧 Step away from the computer.

There's not a lot of peace to be found on that blue, glowing screen. Does repeatedly checking Facebook bring you peace? Or overindulging in horrific news stories? Or spending hours on YouTube?

What other Awesome things have you done? Record your drops here:

💧 _____

_____

_____

💧 _____

_____

_____

💧 _____

_____

_____

COMPOSE A SYMPHONY

Have you ever listened to a gorgeous piece of music or even a catchy pop song and thought, *I wish I could create something like that?* Have you ever created something like that? If so, well done! Then you know it took thousands of tiny Drops of Awesome to accomplish. Maybe your Drops of Awesome will lead you to create musical genius . . . and maybe not. But you can experience the joy of music in a thousand different ways. Try one of these.

 **Sing a song.**

Loud and proud. Even if you're simply providing backup vocals for T-Swift while you drive the preschool carpool, singing is Awesome.

 **Sing a song TO someone in person, in a voicemail, or on the phone.**

 **Teach someone a nursery rhyme.**

 **Pick up an instrument—a kazoo, a guitar, a tambourine, or a piano—and make noise.**

You don't have to actually pick UP the piano to be Awesome.

 **Dance in your car or kitchen.**

 **Pick soothing music to wake you up in the morning.**

 Hum a tune.

Hum IN tune for bonus Awesome points.

 Write down the lyrics to that song you've been writing in your head.

 Whistle while you work.

Invite the mice and birds to join in.

 Thank someone for the music they made.

 Tap out an interesting rhythm on the steering wheel.

This works best if you're the driver.

 Sing a bedtime song.

 Sing in the shower.

Find the music in the world around you.

Close your eyes and pay attention to the sounds of your world: the quissssh *of the garbage truck brakes, the rattle of the wind through the trees, the creaking of your house as it settles in to support your family. Grounding yourself in the sounds of your reality can have a profound calming effect and increase your gratitude, which can, in turn, increase your happiness. The happier you are, the more Awesome you can churn out.*

 Fill glasses with different amounts of water and make music with them.

 Make a new playlist.

Feeling happy? Mellow? Silly? Tall? Choose songs that fit and amplify your mood.

 Shazam that song you like so you can buy it later.

 Put on happy music.

Play some Abba or Queen or the Newsies *soundtrack. Can you stay in a funk when you're rocking out to the musical stylings of the world's largest street-urchin boy band? I rest my case.*

◊ Record the tune you've been humming.

◊ Make a mix CD for a friend.

It's not the '80s, so I'm afraid a mix tape won't get the job done. Share the joy of your favorite songs.

◊ Check your community website for upcoming concerts or musical events.

◊ Join a local band.

After ten years of marriage, my husband, Dan, realized how much he missed playing music with friends, so he found a community band and started to play again. He loves it, and the kids aren't even that mad about having to go to his concerts.

◊ Choose a phone ringtone that lights you up.

I once made a recording of my child singing the ABCs with obvious joy and exuberance—and not necessarily all the right letters—and then turned that into my ringtone.

◊ Clap for a solo.

 Gargle with salt water.

 When someone else starts singing, sing along.

Unless you're at a performance—then probably just listen respectfully.

 Watch a musical.

Deliver your next parenting lecture as a song.

Singing to the tune of her favorite Katy Perry song about how she needs to flush the toilet can only bring you closer together.

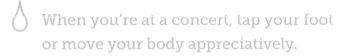 When you're at a concert, tap your foot or move your body appreciatively.

Don't be like my darling children, at ages eight and ten, at their first rock concert. They were all decked out in wizard robes and earplugs, standing in the front row for Harry and the Potters, when I noticed that they were standing stock-still with creepy blank looks on their faces. They were "paying attention," but they were freaking out the band. If you like what the band is playing, smile and MOVE!

Stay for the credits and listen to the music at the end of the movie.

What other Awesome things have you done? Record your drops here:

⬦ _____
   _____
   _____

⬦ _____
   _____
   _____

⬦ _____
   _____
   _____

⬦ _____
   _____
   _____

SAVE A LIFE

You can save a life by actually preventing death or by prolonging life. And what about improving someone else's quality of life and thus preventing it from being wasted in sadness, loneliness, or poor health? You may not know how your choices save someone else, but your positive actions in the world save people in large and small ways every day. And you start by saving or prolonging your own life.

 Go grocery shopping.

Food sustains life. Sustaining life is like saving life.
You go, superhero!

 Rest when you need to.

Let your blood flow and your heart beat.

Pack a snack.

Rather than leaving yourself at the mercy of vending
machines or fast food, keep your car or purse stocked
with simple, healthful food.

Walk to the bus stop.

Buy a houseplant.

Oxygen is good for you. Let a plant exhale fresh air
into your home.

Plan your healthy snacks the night
before.

◊ Drink water.

*There is no system in your body that isn't happier
when it's well hydrated. It can help your digestion,
improve your brain function, reduce back pain,
and give your kidneys a break. Drink and drink and
drink again.*

◊ Make breakfast.

Also, eat it.

◊ Throw an extra vegetable in the next
meal you cook.

◊ Brush your teeth (or even floss, if you're
feeling ambitious).

*Not only does this give you a beautiful, healthy
smile, but some studies show that it can also reduce
your risk of heart disease, possibly adding years to
your life!*

◊ Hold a child's hand to cross the street.

◊ Visit a friend in the hospital.

Listen to someone who needs to talk.

Psst. This means everyone. Some people take longer to open up, so wait patiently for them. Be comfortable with a little bit of silence as you leave space for reluctant talkers to express themselves.

Write a letter to your grandma.

Ask a friend for help.

This saves you and your friend.

Make lunch for you or someone else.

Send an encouraging text.

Tell a friend about an insecurity or failure.

It will bring you closer as friends and show him that no matter how perfect you look on the surface, you struggle, too.

Call a friend to ask how she's doing.

💧 Donate blood.

💧 Put your phone away when you drive.

Don't just put it down—put it out of reach. Taking a quick glance at your incoming text is not important enough to risk hurting yourself or others, but it sure feels like it sometimes. Don't even let it be a temptation.

💧 Baby-proof a cupboard.

💧 Blow on a fluffy dandelion.

This spreads life everywhere. Be careful in which direction you blow.

💧 Signal before you change lanes.

💧 Change an air filter.

💧 Water a plant.

Stop plant dehydration, the silent killer.

◊ Feed a pet.

◊ Send a graduation card.

Sometimes I don't send wedding or graduation cards because I know I can't send cards to everyone I care about for all the special occasions. But isn't it better to celebrate with one friend than to never celebrate at all?

◊ Say out loud the compliments you think about people. ◇

◊ Show up to the wedding reception.

After my first book released, I traveled to several locations for book signings. Places where I had the most friends were often the locations with the worst attendance. Everyone assumed the signings would be packed, so hardly anyone showed up. I spoke to a friend about this, and she said she had a similar experience with her children's wedding receptions; many of their dearest friends did not attend because they assumed they wouldn't be missed. When you can, be the one who shows up. It makes a difference.

◊ Write a joke on someone's lunch napkin. ◇

Make eye contact with and smile at a stranger who seems down.

What other Awesome things have you done? Record your drops here:

_____
_____
_____

_____
_____
_____

_____
_____
_____

_____
_____
_____

ROB THE RICH TO FEED THE POOR

You probably don't want to actually steal, and if you do, I hereby waive all responsibility for said crime. BUT you can choose to take time, stuff, and money from yourself and give it to another person, someone who may need it more than you. Find ways big and small to be generous.

Rip a piece of gum in half and share it.

Put protein bars and water bottles in your car to give to strangers in need.

Offer someone a ride.

Share a magazine when you're done with it. ✧

Host a free garage sale.

There is something fun about getting things to people who need them. Lay out all your garage sale items but price everything as free. It will be fun to see where things end up.

Ask a mom if you can give her daughter a quarter for the horsey ride.

Save a plastic container or jar to take a meal to a friend.

Donate to Goodwill or a local thrift store.

There is something fun about not having to put on a garage sale. Drop off your used bounty and trust that someone will enjoy it.

Pick wildflowers for someone who needs them.

Yes, it's possible to need wildflowers.

Offer to pick something up for a friend while you're grocery shopping.

Lend an egg.

Be the ice cream truck.

Fill a cooler with ice cream, download some ice-cream-truck music, blast it out your car windows, and drive up and down your street giving free ice cream to the kids you know.

Give a kid a penny for a wishing well.

◊ Write *Have a nice day!* on money and let it go on a windy day. ❖

◊ Say "Hi" to the Girl Scouts even if you don't buy cookies from them every single time they offer.

◊ Pray for someone else.

◊ Invite someone to serve with you.

◊ Send a birthday card anytime.

   Even if you missed his birthday, write a note today to tell him you're glad he was born.

◊ Buy wrapping paper from the kid down the street who's selling it for a school fundraiser in hopes of winning herself an inflatable motor scooter.

◊ Buy something from a local small business or farmers' market.

💧 Save all the coins you find around your house and then donate them to a good cause.

💧 Hire a kid to bring in your mail when you're out of town rather than stopping the mail.

Enjoy the look on his face when you pay him two whole dollars per day.

💧 Leave a generous tip.

💧 Refer someone to a good local business.

They will be there with references when you need them if you're there when they need you.

💧 Buy lemonade from the stand.

Drink it, dump it, use it to water your slugs; just buy the lemonade.

💧 Donate some spare canned goods to the food bank.

Contribute to a stranger's groceries.

What other Awesome things have you done? Record your drops here:

_____
_____
_____

_____
_____
_____

_____
_____
_____

_____
_____
_____

EXPLORE THE GALAXY

I'm a little too old, a little too fluffy, and a little too claustrophobic to begin a career as a NASA astronaut, but I do love the feelings of freedom, adventure, and discovery. I just like to experience them without having to drink Tang or pee in a tube.

 Look up hikes near your home.

 Go on a nature walk and notice the life around you.

You'll have to put down your cell phone to accomplish this. #imho #lol

◊ Drive home a different way.

◊ Fold the laundry outside. ◊

Choose not to miss out on a beautiful day just because you have housework.

◊ Ride with the windows down and feel the breeze in your hair.

◊ Find a geocache.

Go to geocaching.com and find out where millions of little treasures are hidden all over the world.

◊ Turn off the radio when you're driving and enjoy the silence.

Explore our galaxy.

The next time you're out on a clear night, take five minutes to look at the stars and see if you can identify any constellations.

Teach someone else how to identify a constellation.

Research museums near where you live.

Browse the nonfiction section of the library and bring home something crazy.

Try a recipe from Pinterest.

They taste way better on your plate than on your computer screen.

Eat something spicy.

Try out a new restaurant.

 Watch a foreign film.

 Wear a glass bubble on your head.

This will help you feel like an astronaut and will inspire conversation with others, thus helping you discover new friends.

 Introduce yourself to a stranger rather than hiding behind your phone or magazine.

 Agree to do something that scares you.

 Start a rock collection.

 Celebrate a crazy new holiday. ◈

SPAM Day? Striped Socks Day? Girls Named Kathryn With Green Eyes Day? Pull out the party poppers!

Really listen to someone instead of thinking about the bajillion things you have to do today/this week. (Especially when you don't really care about what they are saying. Listen because you care about them, and you might even learn something new!) ◆

What other Awesome things have you done? Record your drops here:

○ _____

_____

_____

○ _____

_____

_____

○ _____

_____

_____

WIN AN OSCAR

As a kid, I was in awe of the movie stars working the red carpet. They were beautiful and famous, and they made their fortunes doing what I loved most: being dramatic and creative. I rejoiced with them as they won their awards and imagined it was me. Now that I'm a little older, there's something less than appealing about the idea of being watched all the time, having to care about my image, and never knowing what would be written about me in the tabloids. I would, however, love to spend more time being creative, immersing myself in the arts, focusing on improving my talents, playing dress-up, and receiving recognition.

Make a plan to improve a talent.

If you want to be a better break dancer, write down the steps you'd need to take to accomplish that dream.

1 *Add more core strengthening to your daily exercise routine.*

2 *Watch all the* Step Up *movies in chronological order.*

3 *Buy cooler kicks and sweeter sweatpants.*

4 *Be Awesome.*

 Act less tired than you are.

 Memorize a poem.

 Work harder than you think is possible.

You know your limits, but they're just that, YOUR limits. You decide what they are. When you think you've gone as far as you can go, amaze yourself by taking one more step.

 Work as part of a team.

Try to understand how someone else is feeling.

Read a book.

Start reading a book. You may not start because you don't think you'll have time to finish, but often, if you start, you'll make time to finish. And even if you don't, you'll be a few pages more well read.

Watch a movie that stretches your usual viewing routine.

Write in a journal, even if it's just one sentence per day.

Take time to process your feelings.

There is no happiness without sadness. Let yourself feel sad sometimes. Honor the feeling and work through it rather than trying to skip over it or force it to change.

Perform in a talent show.

 Enter a contest.

Pretend to enjoy your job until you actually start to enjoy it a little more.

Nothing is guaranteed to make me hate writing more than a deadline. It suddenly becomes WORK! On days when I dread my job, I find it helpful to pretend I like it. I'm an actress playing the part of someone who LOVES writing. It reminds me how lucky I am to get paid to do what I love. (Being paid to do it doesn't actually transform the task in any measurable way. All it transforms is my bank account.)

Get dressed for the life you want rather than the life you have.

Spend time looking at yourself in the mirror before you leave for the day.

Sit up straight.

Unless you're a character actor who always plays people with bad posture. Then go right on slouching.

Laugh out loud.

Improve your resting face.

I was once told I have a terrible resting face. A friend said I looked perpetually annoyed. So I reverted back to my high school theater days and started paying more attention to what I do with my face and body language. We give away so many subtle signals about our thoughts and feelings without even realizing what we're doing.

Write a note expressing gratitude and think of it as your acceptance speech.

Audition for a community theater production.

You can become famous in your little town as the third mobster from the left in the local production of Guys and Dolls. You'll make friends and memories and help bring a little culture to your community.

Record a home movie.

Dress up for a grocery trip.

It's not exactly the red carpet, and my cashier rarely asks me "who I'm wearing," but it feels good to glam it up sometimes, even on a day full of mundane tasks.

What other Awesome things have you done? Record your drops here:

⬦ _____
_____
_____

⬦ _____
_____
_____

⬦ _____
_____
_____

⬦ _____
_____
_____

⬦ _____
_____
_____

MAKE YOUR FIRST MILLION

Money can be fantastic or frustrating, and I personally never have a problem spending everything I bring in. I may not be a millionaire, but I can live in abundance if I carefully manage what I have, work a little bit here and there to make a little more, or spend a little less. So you want to make a million dollars? Start with saving one.

◊ Don't buy it, or buy it for someone else.

I often fall in love with things—things I don't need, things I will likely not use. So I take a picture of the item or buy it for a friend that I know will love it, a friend whom I was already planning on shopping for.

◊ Go for a week without spending any money.

◊ Spend money on something joyful and appreciate it.

◊ Declutter your home.

Decluttering can save you money because you see what you have and you don't rebuy something that's lost. Also, after decluttering your home, you are less likely to buy things you don't need and reseed the clutter.

◊ Start or resume a budget.

◊ Pay a bill.

Bonus points: pay a bill on time!

Sell something online.

As you're decluttering, save a few things and try selling them on Craigslist, eBay, or a local Facebook selling group. Be realistic about what you have the time and ability to sell, though. Don't keep your clutter forever with the idea that you'll sell it all someday. Set a time limit. If it's not gone by your chosen day, cart it off to Goodwill.

Invest your money.

Brainstorm business ideas.

Create a rate sheet for services you could offer.

Start a blog.

This may not make money at first—or ever—but if you're willing to put in the work, blogging can be a nice way to earn a little extra income, whether through advertising, affiliate programs, or being paid to blog for commercial sites.

Run a lemonade stand.

○ Start a jar for coins.

○ Compare prices.

○ Read the fine print.

Are you agreeing to purchase cable for one month, or are you selling your soul to Beelzebub for all eternity?

○ Keep track of something good you did at work for your performance review later this year.

○ Save something from your paycheck this month.

○ Ask for a raise.

If you don't ask, the answer is always "No."

○ Print business cards.

◊ Update your résumé.

You may not use it, but it feels good to know you've still got it and can prove it in one page or less.

◊ Take a class.

◊ Make something from scratch.

◊ Reuse something.

Jam jars make great storage containers. Egg cartons work well for planting seedlings. A friend of mine used an old rain gutter as a planter for all her strawberries.

What other Awesome things have you done? Record your drops here:

◊ _____

_____

_____

MAKE AN EPIC COMEBACK

Every hero has her low points, but she uses them as motivation for a comeback rather than letting them swallow her up. Maybe you're at a point where you hop into bed each night and think, *I didn't accomplish anything today*. Well, guess what? You are wrong. Every day, you're doing Awesome things just by being you. Did you breathe in and out all day? Not everyone did—just those who are still with us. Are you still with us? Perfect. Then you are poised for your triumphant hero's comeback. I hope you've always wanted a cheesy movie made about how you triumphed against all odds, because it's go time.

 Create a vision board.

Cut out inspiring pictures from magazines and paste them onto a board to help keep your biggest goals front and center.

 Finish the sentence "I wish I could still . . ." and ask yourself what you'd need to do to make that happen.

 Make a star chart for your good habits.

 Make a list of impossible dreams.

Dreams written down become goals, goals become reality, and reality becomes blog fodder.

 Next time you tell yourself "No," ask yourself "Why not?"

 When you say "Yes," write it down.

Sure, I'm willing to build a life-size model of the solar system to hang at your wedding reception. But if I don't write it down somewhere, it's not happening.

 Do the best you can with what you know now.

 Instead of whining about what's hard, talk about what's possible.

 Set an alarm to remind you to do something.

Writing it down isn't enough? Enlist the help of a bunker-blasting siren on your cell phone to get you out the door for that veterinary Botox appointment.

 Stop apologizing for your messy house, or your ratty car, or your plus-size body.

 Schedule a physical so you can get your body ready for whatever's next.

 Smile while doing something you hate. ❖

Grinning through the green beans helps the antioxidants go down.

Start fresh right now.

Contact someone you haven't spoken to in years.

Check in with a friend to see how one of his goals is coming.

Reward good behavior . . . in yourself.

Positive feedback is a great motivator. But if no one's giving you a cookie, a pat on the back, or a blue ribbon for all the great things you do, take matters into your own hands. Give yourself an air high five or pump your fists and say "Drops of Awesome!" every time you notice yourself being fabulous. And eat a cookie if you must—and you most likely must.

Start a text group in which you and your friends can share all the Awesome things you're doing. ❖

Write down five ways your heartaches have made you stronger.

◊ Congratulate a friend on an accomplishment even if her success makes you feel inadequate.

◊ Start a to-do list.

Even if you don't have the energy to do all the things, you can write down all the things (unless you're graphophobic). Then you might choose one to do!

◊ Start a done list.

If the to-do list seems overwhelming, start tracking what you've done. Sometimes I write down all the things I've done and then cross them off the list.

~~*Work on Drops of Awesome book.*~~

◊ Choose one thing that must be done tomorrow and do it first.

What other Awesome things have you done? Record your drops here:

○ _____
_____
_____

○ _____
_____
_____

○ _____
_____
_____

○ _____
_____
_____

○ _____
_____
_____

PAINT A MASTER-PIECE

Artists see beauty all around them, and they create beauty wherever they go. They capture the goodness they see in the world and share it with others. There are so many ways to increase the world's beauty, be creative, and play with color and shape. Are you doing any of these?

 Sketch something when you have a
spare moment.

Write something on paper.

*This is a lost art in the digital world, but there's
something magical about the feel of your hand
dragging over the paper and the scratch of the pencil
as you create lines and loops to form words and
sentences.*

Doodle.

Write a poem.

Draw a self-portrait.

*Even if it's cartoonish or a stick figure, you will look
back and love what you created. Dan and I once went
on a date where we drew portraits of each other.
Perfect? No. Awesome? Yes.*

Put a pencil and notepad in your purse
or car.

 Excavate your Pinterest mountain by trying one project you pinned.

 Notice the color of the sky.

Is it the same as yesterday? This morning? Last summer in Yellowstone as the sun was setting over the mountains?

 Look through an art book.

 Visit a museum.

 Make art in a public place.

Be creative about making art in a public place— without resorting to vandalism. Use a pressure washer to create art on the sidewalk in front of your house. Gather wildflowers and arrange them on all the benches at the park. Build a sculpture with rocks at the beach. Crochet a hat for a statue on a street corner.

 Set the table beautifully.

○ Fold some origami and leave it for someone as an unexpected gift.

○ Style your hair a new way.

○ Paint a wall.

A baby step toward this is to go to the hardware store and get a few paint samples to try out on your wall. A baby step toward that is to choose a wall in your home that would benefit from being painted.

○ Craft something beautiful to celebrate a holiday.

○ Use the nice glasses at dinner when the only special occasion is that it's Wednesday.

○ Choose a wall hanging to brighten a room.

○ Dust a bookshelf.

 Throw away a piece of clutter.

Think of it as sculpting your home. Remove everything that doesn't belong there and you'll be left with a masterpiece.

 Wear matching socks.

Throw away all your mismatched or worn-out socks.

Take a picture with your phone.

It's never been easier to be an amateur photographer. Rather than clicking away, take twenty seconds to compose your shot in the most artistic way possible.

Put dandelions in a vase.

Add a bracelet to your outfit, even if you're just hanging out at home all day.

Light a candle for no reason at all.

What other Awesome things have you done? Record your drops here:

⬦ _____

_____

_____

⬦ _____

_____

_____

⬦ _____

_____

_____

⬦ _____

_____

_____

⬦ _____

_____

_____

RAISE A HAPPY FAMILY

Raising a family full of happy, successful people is one of the most epic achievements possible and one that so many of us aspire to. Do we think it's really achievable? Are we giving ourselves enough credit for the thousands of things we do to make this a reality? Whether we're raising our own kids or contributing to the lives of others, we can all support families and, consequently, change the world for the better.

💧 Ask the kids to help around the house.

You mean you get Drops of Awesome for enforced child labor? Yes. Yes, you do.

💧 Serve someone together.

💧 Ignore the attitude.

Sometimes you just need to ignore the bad attitude and treat him as if he were all sunshine and roses. Do you ever have a bad attitude? How would it feel to be called on it every single time?

💧 Buy her the gum before she asks, and then thank her for not begging for gum.

💧 Explain that you don't buy certain things because they're not in the budget.

💧 Leave notes on their pillows expressing gratitude for the small things they think no one noticed. ✦

 Let a child plan the day. ❖

Take a note from the old acting improvisation game, "Yes, and . . ."

"Mom, can we go to the park today?" "Yes, and . . . shall we see if Henry wants to come, too?"

 Give a hug.

Encourage him to try his best.

It doesn't have to be THE best. It just needs to be HIS best.

Speak kindly about someone who's difficult to love.

Tell her she's beautiful.

Whisper words of love when he's asleep.

Maybe they aren't receptive when they're awake. Sneak into their rooms at night and whisper all the loving things you want them to know.

◊ Run outside with your kids when it starts to rain and dance with them. ◇

◊ Help a child who wakes you in the night.

Bonus points if you remember her name while you're helping her.

◊ Read a story to a child.

◊ Flush the toilet for them.

◊ Teach them to flush the toilet.

If you've figured out how to do this one, please leave instructions at www.dropsofawesome.com/forthelovewilltheyeverlearntoflush.

◊ Eat ice cream for breakfast in the summer. ◇

◊ Cook a meal.

 Order dessert.

 Start a holiday tradition.

This doesn't have to be elaborate. Usually, it's best if it's not.

 Sing "Happy Birthday."

 Fill out a field trip form.

 Sit down and talk with a teacher about your child.

 Play a game together.

I can think of no better way to get my family members all talking and laughing with each other. I had to play a lot of super lame games in the early years to train them to later play the games I actually enjoy playing, but it was totally worth it and we've had a ton of fun along the way.

 Have a discussion about honesty.

 Turn off the radio and talk to your passengers while you're driving.

 Stop and look—really look—at a person or a place.

 *Form a memory you won't forget. Everything changes, but don't you want to always remember the way she shivered when she ate green beans or how it felt to listen to him play that super repetitive song on the violin?*

Turn off your devices.

Go for a family walk.

This doesn't have to be with a pickax up Everest. Around the block will do quite nicely.

Pick up a work shift for a mom or dad who needs time off to be with one of their kids.

Show love to a child who needs it, whether she's yours or not.

◊ Evaluate.

After a fun outing or even after a fight, talk it over with your family. How did that go? What did we do well? What could we have done differently? What did we learn?

◊ Don't evaluate everything to death.

What other Awesome things have you done? Record your drops here:

◊ _____

_____

_____

◊ _____

_____

_____

◊ _____

_____

_____

BUILD YOUR DREAM HOUSE

I've always thought it would be cool to build my own home from the ground up. I'd learn how to wire it and nail things with one of those electronical nailer mallets. Once I was finished, I'd take such Awesome pride and joy in the house that Kate built.

Realistically, I may not ever build a house, but there are a ton of things I can do or am already doing to build up my house, to make my living space more livable, and to develop pride and joy in the place where I rest my bones.

Deal with your mail today the first time you touch it.

Declutter two things from a drawer.

Make one thing better in the room you're in.

Every time you walk through a room, make it one Drop cleaner, more organized, or more joyful.

Smile while you clean the house.

Put an item back when you're done with it.

Sweep your front porch.

Clean as you go. ✧

There are very few jobs so epic that you can't clean up after yourself as you go, even if you think you're too tired. Consider it your gift to your future self.

💧 Carry something with you to put away as you head downstairs.

💧 Put the Lego in the bin before you step on it again.

💧 Rinse your dish and load it into the dishwasher when you finish eating.

💧 Clean the space you have.

I recently saw an anonymous quote that said, "Rather than complaining that the grass is greener, focus on improving your own yard." You may not have the home you always dreamed of, but you can make the most of the space you have. Make it as beautiful as your budget will allow. Keep it as clean as your sanity can handle.

💧 Scrub one shower wall each time you're in it. Throw the floor into the rotation and the shower will stay magically clean.

Pick up that stray sock in the corner.

 Build an AWESOME tissue mountain.

Next time you have a cold, see how large of a tissue mountain you can create on the floor beside your bed. Of course, you'll need to excavate it when your health has returned.

 Buff a faucet until it shines.

 Don't wait until it's time to sell to fix up the house.

Looking at your house and your budget, see what things you can afford to fix now so you can enjoy them yourself. If it helps, pretend you're getting ready to put your house on the market.

 Become a YouTube contractor.

You can learn everything—from how to install a garbage disposal to how to brew your own moonshine—on the magical World Wide Web. So before you hire a contractor, do a quick search and see how easy it is.

◊ Replace a light fixture.

◊ Make your bed with clean sheets.

◊ Make a simple household cleaner.

One part vinegar, two parts water, and several drops of your favorite essential oil. Cheap, easy, and it smells amazing.

◊ Build or repair a fence.

◊ Patch a wall.

I've been overwhelmed by this job, and holes have been known to live for years unpatched on my walls. Breaking it down into steps makes it more doable. Maybe today, you just gather the supplies. Tomorrow, you putty the hole. The next day, you sand it and retexture the wall. Eventually, the paint may need to come out, but that's DAYS away. Today, you're just gathering a few supplies.

What other Awesome things have you done? Record your drops here:

⬦ _____
_____
_____
_____

⬦ _____
_____
_____
_____

⬦ _____
_____
_____
_____

⬦ _____
_____
_____
_____

⬦ _____
_____
_____
_____

CURE CANCER

This horrible disease has affected my family multiple times, and I donate and I hope and pray that someday a cure will be found. The joy in this accomplishment comes from saving lives, solving a problem, righting a great wrong, helping someone, and improving world health. You don't have to solve all the problems—just pick one.

Want to help, even if you don't know what to do.

Sometimes I feel sick inside because there are so many causes I want to help with but no humanly possible way for me to do it all. However, there is something to be said for having good desires and a willingness to help wherever we can.

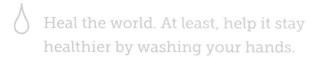

Heal the world. At least, help it stay healthier by washing your hands.

Teach nutrition.

Whether through example or outright indoctrination, share what you know about healthy eating.

Take something healthful to a potluck dinner.

Visit a farmers' market.

Load up on fresh fruits and vegetables and free-range donuts while feeling good about reducing waste and supporting your neighbors.

 Donate to an important cause.

Like a cause on Facebook.

If you don't have the money to donate, promoting a cause online could encourage someone else to donate.

If you can't say something nice, don't say anything.

Intend to be there.

Intentions matter. Did you miss an important appointment? Did you want to be there? Give yourself credit for your intentions.

Take a break when you're tired and then try again.

Dedicate an hour to completing a task you've been procrastinating.

Forgive yourself.

Harsh self-criticism and blame are like a cancer, causing stress and building on themselves. The worse I feel about myself, the more I notice all the ways I suck at life. The good news is that the reverse is true: the more you forgive yourself and acknowledge what you're doing right, the more ways you will notice you're killing it. And if you start to identify yourself as a champion, you'll be more likely to do things on the Awesome end of the spectrum.

 Focus on the nice people.

 Procrastinate laziness.

We all want to chill out and be lazy sometimes. Next time you find yourself wanting to surrender your productivity to the couch, procrastinate your lazination for five minutes. I'm Awesome at procrastinating, so this one works well for me.

 Turn off the television.

 Focus on what you can do to improve your life rather than thinking about how someone else has it better than you.

Be real. ◇

It is refreshing to be in a conversation with someone who speaks with candor and not just politically correct politeness. Be that person who speaks truth in a matter-of-fact way, no matter how inelegant.

W hat other Awesome things have you done? Record your drops here:

_____

_____

_____

_____

_____

_____

_____

_____

_____

EXPERIENCE THE GREATEST LOVE OF ALL

Unlike what we've been taught by our favorite romantic comedies and our secretly devoured, post-apocalyptic, hormonal-teen-vampire novels, love does not simply attack you like a Mr. Darcy in the night. You have to work at it. And there are so many kinds of love we can cultivate. If you want a little more friendship, respect, love, passion, or romance in your life, try some of these.

Stop the next negative comment before it leaves your mouth.

Negative comments are draining and generally unproductive. Spending ten minutes complaining about how rudely customer service treated you won't fill anyone up with joy. When you speak, bring the joy.

 Just listen.

 Apologize.

 Don't call with bad news when not necessary.

When I'm upset, I want to commiserate with someone. So I developed a habit of calling my husband every time something bad happened, regardless of where he was or what he was doing. Avocados were outrageously expensive. Brrringggg. Our child got a bad grade on a report card. Brrringggg. My plants look depressed. Brrringggg. Imagine how excited he was every time his caller ID showed my name. (I'm working to change this.)

 Win at kindness. ◇

 Notice what he's doing right.

Hug her hello.

It feels amazing to come home and instantly feel loved and wanted. Next time she comes home, stop what you're doing the second she comes in the door and greet her with a crushing embrace.

Go for a walk with someone you love.

Ask the name of her dog.

Say something nice about his kid.

How much do you love the people who love your people? The easiest way to become my lifelong friend is to show kindness to or speak kindly about my spouse or one of my kids.

Wave to the garbage man.

Hold eye contact for a little longer than you're comfortable with.

 Commiserate with the cashier.

"This line is long. They should get you more help. I hope you get a break soon. You're doing a great job."

 Give chocolate to a friend. ◆

◊ Give chocolate to yourself.

◊ Schedule a date with yourself. ◆

When you're feeling down, spend time getting to know yourself, recharging, and feeling your feels. Take yourself to a movie, out to dinner, on a hike, or to a hammock with a book. Make it restorative, meaningful, and fun.

 Write down reasons you love him.

◊ Give him the list.

◊ Compliment her to someone else.

This is even better if she's around to hear you sing her praises.

 Hold hands.

 Kiss him goodbye.

 Ask her about something she cares about.

"How did your new shoes feel at soccer practice?" "Did your boss get back from vacation?" "Are you getting excited for the polka rave this weekend?"

 Give up doing something you love so he can do something he wants to do.

 Cue up a shmoopy love song to play in her car the next time she starts it.

 Plan a date night.

Maybe you go on dates all the time. Plan something special; it doesn't need to cost a fortune. Find somewhere you can watch the sunset. Play romantic music in the car on your way to the bowling alley. Make a special effort to hold his hand more than usual. Purposely smell good.

 Snuggle.

 Dress up nicely.

For a spouse, this shows him that you're still trying to win him over like when you were dating. For a friend, this shows that you care enough about the time you spend together to be at your best. For a child, this makes you slightly less embarrassing when you stop by the school.

 Think about her when she's not around.

Write a love note.

I like to hide these in unexpected places: the microwave, the shower, under the wiper blade on his windshield in a parking ticket envelope.

W

hat other Awesome things have you done? Record your drops here:

⬦ _____
_____
_____

⬦ _____
_____
_____

⬦ _____
_____
_____

⬦ _____
_____
_____

⬦ _____
_____
_____

START A NONPROFIT

Are you ready to be the next Bill or Melinda Gates? I love the way they see a problem and systematically look for a solution. People who achieve great things that make a difference in the world have focus and direction. They think about how their actions affect others. They make plans and they follow through. Can you add a Drop of planning, focus, positivity, or follow-through to your life?

💧 Check your calendar for tomorrow before going to bed tonight.

Have you ever forgotten an appointment because you failed to look at your calendar? Me neither . . .

💧 Arrive five minutes early.

💧 Shake hands with a stranger.

💧 Make a list of the things you are most passionate about.

Post it where you can see it every day, and your brain will start working on ways you can be more involved in the things that matter most to you.

💧 Choose ways to share that passion with others.

💧 Leave the next conversation you're in one Drop more positive because you participated.

○ Daydream about ways you could improve the world around you.

As you plan to be and do good, you will find yourself confronted with opportunities to put those dreams into action.

○ Choose one thing in which to lead by example.

○ Volunteer in the community or at a food pantry, or go to volunteermatch.org to find a new opportunity to serve.

○ Look around for the needs of others.

Do you know someone who always seems to notice what you need? I am amazed by these people. It starts by opening your eyes and noticing one need. Focus on one person in your life—a child or a spouse—and ask yourself what he or she needs.

○ Choose a need to fill.

Now that you've got your ticket for the Train of Compassionate Observation, ride it all the way to Do Something About It Station.

○ Volunteer at a local school even if you don't have a child who attends there.

○ Join the PTA.

○ Invite friends to volunteer with you.

○ Call your political representative.

I spent much of my life thinking I couldn't call a legislator to ask for education to be fully funded because I didn't understand the entire budget and all the implications of the financial decisions he was making. But when I was serving as the legislative chair for my local PTA, I found out that my state legislators are lobbied constantly by various special interest groups and that they keep records of all the calls they receive to give them an idea of how much support they have for various initiatives. If I call and say, "Please make education a financial priority," that's one tally mark in the box for people who care about education. I don't need to understand the intricacies of the budget; I just need to speak out as one voice that cares about education. It makes a difference.

○ Donate used books to the library.

○ Gather other people's used books and take them to the library.

○ Pay library fines.

I like to think that I forget to return my library books on purpose because I want to be one of the library's biggest financial supporters.

○ Use your employer's donation matching when you give to charitable organizations.

○ Ask a shelter if they need your old blankets.

○ Take school supplies to a teacher.

○ Mow a neighbor's yard.

"Oops. Did I cut all of your grass again? I hope you didn't need it for anything."

◊ Offer to babysit a friend's child for free.

◊ Sweep a neighbor's porch.

Dust the cobwebs, sweep the dirt, shake off the mat. Ten points if you can do it without getting caught.

◊ Speak up for a coworker in a meeting.

◊ Sacrifice your time to take your child to sports or other activities.

◊ Wave at the construction sign holder.

No one likes being stuck in construction traffic, and I'm sure the guy holding the stop sign that's kept you waiting for fifteen minutes when you're already late for your dental appointment isn't getting a ton of love from the people he's stopping. Smile and wave as you pass.

What other Awesome things have you done? Record your drops here:

◊ _____
_____
_____

◊ _____
_____
_____

◊ _____
_____
_____

◊ _____
_____
_____

◊ _____
_____
_____

DISCOVER A NEW SPECIES

Get out your khakis and sun hat and make sure your malaria shots are up to date. It's time to spend months in the jungle counting toad warts. Not your cup of tea? Here are a few Awesome activities to help you connect with nature, discover something new, or care for living things.

Plant a seed and watch it grow.

One of my favorites to plant is wheatgrass, bringing me springtime any time of year. Fill containers with dirt and sprinkle them with wheat berries purchased from somewhere that doesn't use desiccant packets in their storage containers. Water and enjoy the bright springy greens growing right inside your home. They're great for decoration or as Easter grass and fabulous in a smoothie.

 Listen to bird songs.

 Pet a dog.

 Plant wildflowers.

Along a local freeway entrance ramp, someone planted wildflower seeds that grew into thousands of gorgeous flowers that return each year. This is an easy way to turn something ugly into something beautiful. (You may need to ask permission first.)

 Feed the ducks.

 Ride a horse.

◊ Give birth to a child.

This will take at least nine months of advance planning, but it will give you years of opportunities to discover a completely new and unique creature.

◊ Take a new path on your walk and make friends with an interesting tree.

◊ Go camping.

◊ Adopt a pet from a shelter.

◊ Rejoice in the differences of others.

Rather than being scared of differences, be curious. Ask someone to tell you his or her story.

◊ Take a whiff! Enjoy the scent of the outdoors.

◊ Take a nature photo in an unlikely place.

◊ Visit a park.

You don't need to have a kid or be a kid to go to the park. Swing on a swing, lay in the grass, make a daisy chain, or sit on a bench and feel the breeze whispering about how you slaughter at recreating.

◊ Turn over a rock to see what's living underneath.

◊ Play "I Spy."

I recently played this with my daughter as we were speeding along in our car, and she spied something green. I guessed that it was a tree. It WAS! "Now guess WHICH tree it is," she said. A game of discovery, indeed. Next time we play, I may have her guess which specific blade of grass I spy.

◊ Go fishing.

◊ Visit a zoo if you don't have room for giraffes or caribou in your yard.

◊ Share a cool discovery online.

◊ Order something completely new at a restaurant.

If you're feeling adventurous, have everyone at the table order someone else's meal.

◊ Invent a new nickname for a friend.

◊ Throw greens into your smoothie.

◊ Try a natural health remedy.

Essential oil, herbal tea, acupressure. Whether they work for your body or not, it feels good to do something that sends your body the message that you're willing to care for it.

◊ Let a bug live.

◊ Guess the weather by looking at cloud formations.

◊ Mow your grass.

 Clean out a drawer of your refrigerator.

If yours is like mine, there's a good chance you'll discover some new "life" in there. Be sure to disinfect.

Invite someone over who's never been to your house before.

Pick one weed.

An overwhelming mess of weeds ups my blood pressure, but if I just pick one or two every time I walk by, I can keep my garden beds looking decent, and it doesn't have to be a big project.

What other Awesome things have you done? Record your drops here:

⬭ _____
   _____
   _____

⬭ _____
   _____
   _____

⬭ _____
   _____
   _____

⬭ _____
   _____
   _____

⬭ _____
   _____
   _____

START A RELIGIOUS MOVEMENT

There are so many faith traditions in the world that sometimes it's hard to see a common thread. However, most people get their worship on for similar reasons. We want to feel peace, to spread goodness, and to honor something greater than ourselves. This is an area where sometimes the tiniest efforts make a huge difference.

Meditate when you wake up before you do anything else.

Try breathing in and out for five minutes with your eyes closed, focusing your attention on the path your breath travels. In and out. It's hard to clear your mind of all thought and just be. Breathing gives you something to focus on besides your own hamster wheel of worries and to-dos.

 Watch a sunrise.

 Spend five minutes thinking about what you truly believe.

 Choose one day each week to rest.

 Be still.

I once had a meditation teacher encourage me to take time every day to sit still, breathe, and wait until I could feel love. He encouraged me to stop frantically seeking peace and to just sit and let peace find me.

 Say a prayer.

 Breathe through your fear or anger.

 List your blessings.

 Focus on the good, the joy, the miracles.

Are you alive to read this? Do you have the ability to move, to laugh, to love? Do you have shelter, food to eat, and clean water to drink? Do you frequently go out into the world without being hurt, mocked, or mistreated in any way? While you were reading the last sentence, did you not get skidooshed by a meteor? Then you have a great life.

Read an uplifting article or book.

Tell someone you love them.

Write out a favorite quote or verse of scripture and hang it on your mirror.

Make spirituality a priority by scheduling devotional time.

○ Schedule a conversation with a religious leader.

Regardless of denomination, take advantage of the wisdom of someone who has spent years of his life counseling people to live lives of goodness.

○ Research churches, synagogues, or meditation classes in your area.

○ Attend a worship service or meeting.

○ Post something spiritually uplifting on Instagram or Facebook.

Be the opposite of the serial-inflammatory-political- or news-footage poster. (You know you have one in your feed.) Post something that inspires people to be better, more honest, more productive, more kind, or more noble.

○ Write down some inspiration.

○ Teach a class or share your feelings with a group.

Tell someone if you're struggling.

Whether physically, emotionally, spiritually, or mentally, everyone struggles. Talking about it can be so freeing, and it can also help the person you're confiding in as they see that they're not alone in their struggles and as they forget themselves and help you.

 Tell someone what you've learned.

 When someone wishes you a happy Hanukkah, Christmas, or Ramadan, wish them the same, regardless of your religious beliefs.

 Hold in a negative or sarcastic comment that would make people laugh at someone else's expense and possibly hurt him. ◇

 Write a Christmas letter.

What other Awesome things have you done? Record your drops here:

○ _____
_____
_____

○ _____
_____
_____

○ _____
_____
_____

○ _____
_____
_____

○ _____
_____
_____

ARREST A CRIMINAL

My brother is a United States federal agent. He brings down bad guys and sometimes rides in helicopters while carrying large weapons. I want to be him when I grow up, but I probably won't. However, there are things I can do to be Awesome by promoting goodness, health, and safety in my community.

Close your neighbor's mailbox (that the postal worker accidentally left open) to protect the mail that's inside.

Teach a child how to cross the street safely.

Then teach him again. And then one or twenty more times for good measure.

Cross at a crosswalk.

Drive all the way to the grocery store without speeding.

Drive on the road rather than on the sidewalk.

Help a child who looks lost.

I am loath to admit how many times one of my children has been that lost child, and a kind stranger has always noticed her distress and helped her find me. I want to be that person.

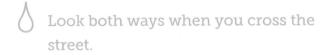

Renew your vehicle license on time.

Look both ways when you cross the street.

Take an item to the lost and found.

I take the dumbest things to the lost and found because I've been the mother of the child who lost her favorite gray Lego brick, Barbie sock, or broken key chain and begged me to look all over the museum for it. If I find an equally precious treasure, I turn it in.

Stop the crime of littering by picking up a piece of trash at the park.

Use your Sharpie to write on paper rather than on the bathroom stall.

Leave the beach cleaner than you found it.

⬦ Take cookies to the officers at the police station.

⬦ Ask someone in the community if you can help them with anything.

> *One year, my family did an act of service for someone different in the community every day during the month of December. (Notice I said one year—not every year.) One of the days, we called up the fire station and asked what we could do to help them. We ended up wiping down tables in an instruction room. It was a small thing, but it made a difference, and my kids remember that we helped the people who help us.*

⬦ Call 911 to report a drunk driver.

⬦ Continue to commit all the tiny acts of lawfulness that have become second nature, like refraining from selling illegal drugs or choosing not to rob the next bank you see.

⬦ Attend a community concert or event.

 Clear a trail.

Look up your local hiking or trail association and see when their next work party will be held.

 Use a community park.

Extinguish your campfire all the way.

Help an Eagle Scout complete his project.

Participate in the National Day of Service and Remembrance.

In the United States, it's on September 11, and most communities have projects available. If there's not one near you, start your own.

Host a neighborhood potluck.

Put up a flag in support of something: a country, a team, a political candidate, an ice cream flavor.

◊ Wish a police officer a good day.

◊ Say something kind or respectful about a public servant you disagree with.

◊ Pay your parking tickets.

◊ Vote.

◊ Be honest on your taxes.

What other Awesome things have you done? Record your drops here:

◊ _____
_____
_____

EARN A COLLEGE DEGREE

Earning a college degree gives you a magical piece of paper that can open doors to broader employment opportunities. It says, "This person has special skills and knows how to complete something." But for me, even more important than making me more marketable, earning a college degree opened my mind to all kinds of thoughts and ideas and taught me how to learn. I also proved to myself that I could do hard things. I may never actually go back to school and earn an advanced degree, but I can be a perpetual student—always learning, always experiencing new things.

Read a page of a magazine.

I will never finish all the magazines lying around my house, and sometimes that thought causes me to avoid picking them up at all. But just because I may not be able to read all 150 pages doesn't mean I can't learn something new by thumbing through and reading a page or two.

Visit a library.

Follow a link to an educational article.

As fascinating as it may be to read about some celebrity's botched plastic surgery, your time might be better spent reading about how to get your garden to yield more radishes or how glue works.

Read a newspaper.

Put a book in your car so you're always prepared to learn.

Attend a concert that exposes you to a new kind of music.

⬙ Read about your town.

Is there a local historical society? Explore one of their publications to learn about where you live.

⬙ Choose a nonfiction book to read at the beach.

⬙ Write something in your neatest handwriting.

⬙ Read the trail signs on your hike.

Why do they call that plant "Devil's Club"? How many pumas live in this park? Do the fungi here really taste like cotton candy?

⬙ Learn a new language a word at a time.

⬙ Identify a tree.

Bob? Is that you?

⬙ Help a child learn a skill.

○ Sign up for a class at the library, the community college, or the gym.

○ Write a list of things you want to learn how to do.

○ Make a plan.

I recently took a position on a nonprofit board of directors. I planned to attend our first meeting, but I wrote it on my calendar for the wrong day. When I realized I'd missed it, I was mortified, but rather than wallowing in my embarrassing, loserly failure, I apologized and decided to focus on making a plan so I wouldn't repeat my mistake. You can't change the past, but the future is up for grabs, so move on and plan to improve.

○ Schedule time for learning on your calendar.

○ Keep improving.

Don't be afraid of your faults. They just give you obstacles to overcome.

⬦ Read to someone else.

⬦ Ask another person what they've learned this week.

⬦ Ask yourself *why* you're doing something.

Look at the way you eat, the way you sit, and the shows you watch on TV and then think about why you do it. Is it what you want to be doing with your body, your time, or your money?

What other Awesome things have you done? Record your drops here:

⬦ _____

_____

_____

⬦ _____

_____

_____

INVENT
A NEW
TECHNOLOGY

I've always wanted to go down to my secret laboratory and create something amazing that would change the world. Maybe, like me, you're not a mad scientist. That's okay! You can still create something new, solve a problem, learn how things work, or figure out how to make them work yourself. You're on your road to invention!

◊ Walk through each room of your house and write down what needs to be fixed.

"Need" is a funny word. How about writing down all the things you'd like to fix whether they are actual "needs" or not?

◊ File something.

◊ Put training wheels on a bike, pump up a tire, or grease a chain.

◊ Find the solution to one problem.

I hang the charging cords to my devices from the knobs of my dresser. It's super annoying because when they're plugged in, it's hard to access my drawers. Recently, a friend walked through my room, pointed to the mess of cords, and said, "You should hang those from the side of the dresser with a sticky hook." Bam. Three-year problem, solved. Choose one thing that's bothering you and come up with a creative solution.

◊ Reuse an old shoe box or food container for home storage.

 Fix a leaky faucet.

 Check the oil in your car.

 Choose a place for your keys to go.
Every time.

*This little innovation probably saves me several
hours per year, when in the past I would have
been searching for my unlocking and driving
implements.*

 Build something.

 Assess the workflow in your kitchen.

*Is there an item in your kitchen that annoys you
every time you have to retrieve it? If you're bending
low to get your lids ten times a day, consider
moving them to more convenient real estate. The
Power Rangers inflatable beer steins can possibly be
relocated to somewhere more out of the way.*

 Organize your purse.

Put a trash bag in your car.

I invented this. You're welcome.

 Read a book about technology.

What are microwaves? How do the tiny genius robots in your computer box make the screen of viewing light up? These and other magical mysteries can be unfolded to you in the pages of a good old-fashioned book.

 Take apart an old appliance to see how it works.

 Clean out your email inbox.

 Write some code.

Dan does the bulk of the code writing here, but I've had fun messing around with basic HTML. It really gets the nerd juice flowing through my veins.

 Use what's in your fridge to cook something new without a recipe.

💧 Learn a new computer program or how to do something new in an old one.

Have you ever watched someone do something amazing in Word or Notepad and thought, "I've used that program for ten years and I never knew it could do that!"? Well, it can't do that until you learn how. So explore a little more or take a tutorial.

💧 Assemble some furniture.

💧 Put together a jigsaw puzzle.

💧 Buy a pocket protector.

At least you'll look like an inventor.

💧 Fill a spray bottle with cold water on a hot day and spritz people with it.

💧 Clean the crumbs out of your toaster.

You will be upgrading to a device that does not set off the smoke alarm.

What other Awesome things have you done? Record your drops here:

○ _____
_____
_____

○ _____
_____
_____

○ _____
_____
_____

○ _____
_____
_____

○ _____
_____
_____

WIN AN OLYMPIC MEDAL

I wouldn't personally enjoy the life of an elite athlete—drinking raw egg yolks, doing chin-ups, waking up at stupid o'clock in the morning, and posing for Wheaties boxes. (That's what they do, right?) But I could use better health, discipline, and focus and a stronger sense of teamwork.

 **Drop and give me ten.**

Push-ups, sit-ups, planks . . . cookies?

 **Drink water.**

Practice yoga.

Keep breathing.

Some days, this is easier than others. If there's nothing else you can do, just keep breathing in and out. Focus on that breathing, be grateful for that breath, and keep it coming!

Plan an active family vacation.

March while you stir the soup.

Get up off the couch.

March in place, pick up one thing in your house, or take a walk around your living room. If you've been sitting in one place so long that you're leaving a person-shaped indent, take a break from taking a break.

💧 Get out of bed.

You already did it yesterday? Do it again.

💧 Do five calf raises on your way out of bed in the morning, rising up on your tiptoes and dropping down again.

💧 Pretend to like mornings.

A dear friend had always hated mornings until one day she decided to just fake it, to pretend she liked mornings. She said it took just a few months of pasting on a smile as she shlumped out of bed and, eventually, she grew to be a morning person.

💧 Actually like mornings.

💧 Get up five minutes earlier than you need to.

Enjoy the stillness or at least appreciate the coolness of your pillow before you get up.

💧 Take the stairs instead of the elevator.

 Walk to a friend's house nearby that you would normally drive to.

 Take a nap.

There is nothing more Awesome. Nappers are the best sort of people.

 Race to the mailbox.

 Jog in place.

 Bike to work.

If you work from home, maybe bike to someone else's workplace—like the gelato maker's, for example.

 Do jumping jacks at road trip rest stops.

 Take a five-minute walk.

 Stretch.

Listen to your body.

If it says "Slow down," slow down. If it says "Drink water," drink water. If it says "Touch your elbow," touch your elbow, but only if Simon also says.

Think of exercise as a reward.

Sign up for an athletic event.

There's nothing that motivates me to exercise and get fit more than paying money to be part of an event. The couch is calling my name, but I paid five dollars to enter that race. I'd better get moving.

Create an athletic event.

Invite friends and family to participate in a race. If you have the money, make T-shirts. Make it fun.

Eat a new vegetable.

Eat an old vegetable.

Drink water again.

Plan a healthy dinner.

If you like this, plan a week of healthy dinners. If you like THAT, plan a month of healthy dinners and reuse it over and over again, replacing meals as you get bored.

 Set one nonnegotiable goal.

Olympic athletes dream big and set big goals, and they don't waver. You cannot turn every single thing in your life into a nonnegotiable goal—but pick one. Have one thing you are totally committed to and never give up. If you miss one day of your nonnegotiable, make it nonnegotiable again tomorrow.

 Try again. ◇

 Take a class.

I took adult hip hop, and it was more hilarious than hardcore, but I had the best time and got some great blackmail photos of my girlfriends.

What other Awesome things have you done? Record your drops here:

◊ _____
_____
_____
_____

◊ _____
_____
_____
_____

◊ _____
_____
_____
_____

◊ _____
_____
_____
_____

◊ _____
_____
_____
_____

CONCLUSION

You made it through! Do you feel more Awesome? I sure hope so. The magic of Drops of Awesome is that when you find yourself drifting into negativity, you can pick right up where you got off track and try again. And again. Every minute of every day is the perfect minute to recognize what you're doing right or to add one more Drop of Awesome to your Bucket.

Don't let your fears or your past or your physical limitations or your unrealistic expectations stop you from doing one more good thing today. You deserve to be motivated by your own brilliance.

Go forth.

Be Awesome.

ACKNOWLEDGMENTS

Thanks to my family, the Familius team, KayLynn for the editing help, and all my friends who live in the world and on the Internet for their continued friendship and encouragement on DropsofAwesome.com and the Drops of Awesome Facebook page.

ABOUT FAMILIUS

Welcome to a place where heart is at the center of our families, and family at the center of our homes. Where boo-boos are still kissed, cake beaters are still licked, and mistakes are still okay. Welcome to a place where books—and family—are beautiful. Familius: a book publisher dedicated to helping families be happy.

VISIT OUR WEBSITE: WWW.FAMILIUS.COM

Our website is a different kind of place. Get inspired, read articles, discover books, watch videos, connect with our family experts, download books and apps and audiobooks, and along the way, discover how values and happy family life go together.

GET BULK DISCOUNTS

If you feel a few friends and family might benefit from what you've read, let us know and we'll be happy to provide you with quantity discounts. Simply email us at specialorders@familius.com.

- Website: www.familius.com
- Facebook: www.facebook.com/paterfamilius
- Twitter: @familiustalk, @paterfamilius1
- Pinterest: www.pinterest.com/familius

THE MOST IMPORTANT WORK YOU EVER DO WILL
BE WITHIN THE WALLS OF YOUR OWN HOME.